THIS COLORING BOOK BELONGS
TO LITTLE ARTIST

_____

HELLO, LITTLE ARTIST!

How to use this coloring book:

- Start by reimagining and coloring the cover on the right in your unique way. :)
- Flood the pages with colors, doodles and wonder!
- There are over 80 stickers in the middle of the book. Each design can be found somewhere in the book. Match stickers with their images or just place them randomly on the pages, where you think they'll look prettier.

Happy imagining and happy exploring!

With vibrant smudges,
Your worldwide buddies

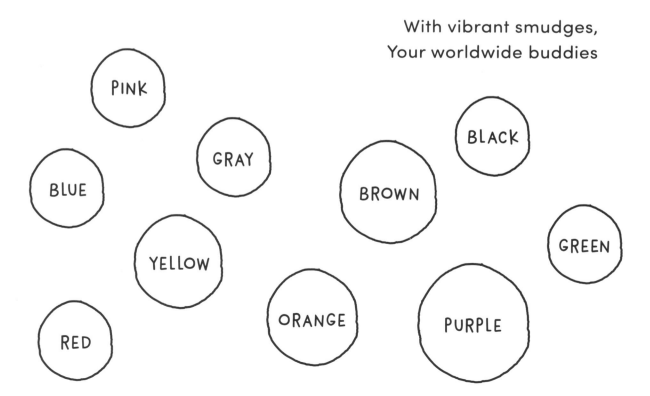

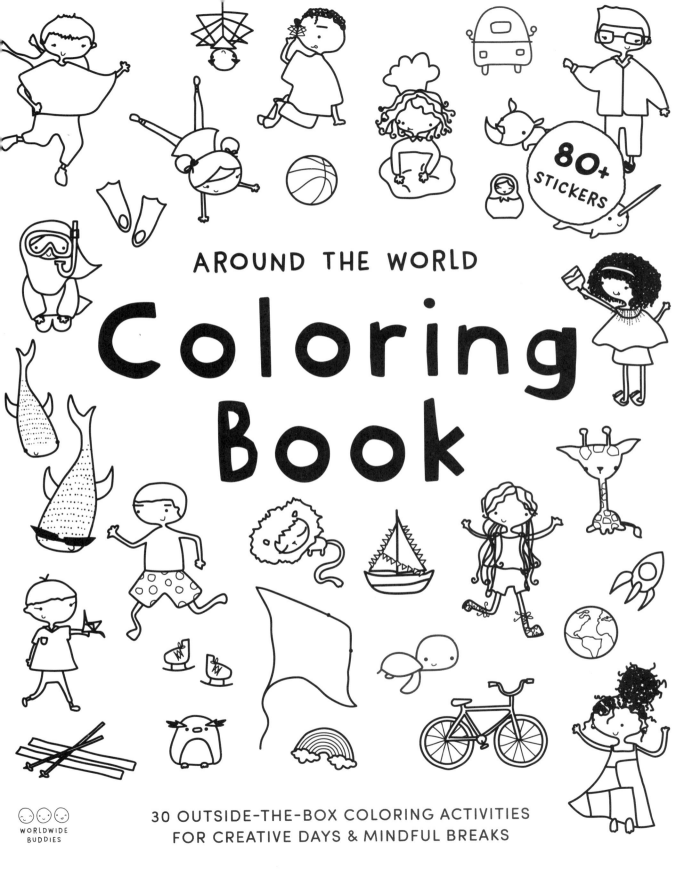

AROUND THE WORLD

Coloring Book

80+ STICKERS

30 OUTSIDE-THE-BOX COLORING ACTIVITIES
FOR CREATIVE DAYS & MINDFUL BREAKS

WORLDWIDE BUDDIES

The world is a beautiful
place filled with wonder!
Color it in and name the country
where each buddy lives.
You can even match each continent
with its name and decorate it
with a different pattern.

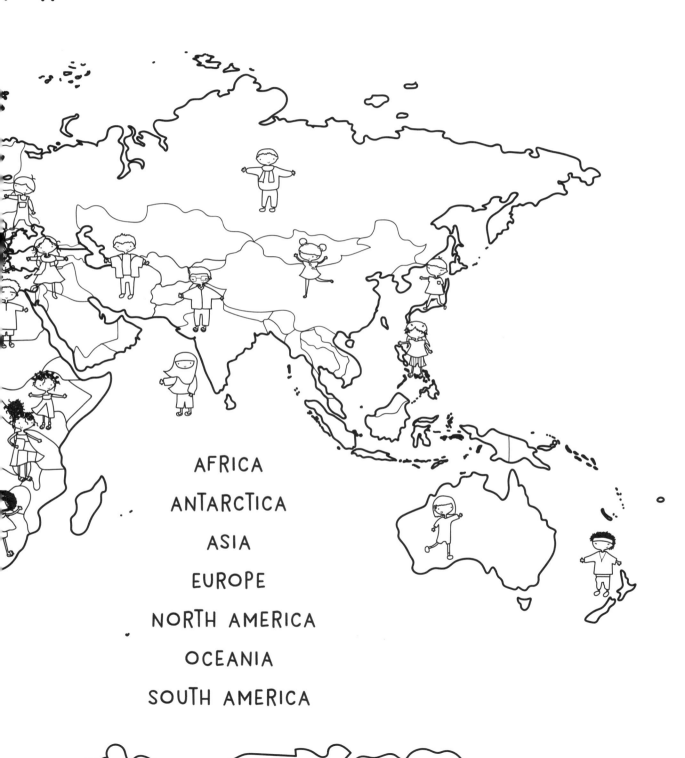

AFRICA

ANTARCTICA

ASIA

EUROPE

NORTH AMERICA

OCEANIA

SOUTH AMERICA

MATRYOSHKA DOLLS

Matryoshka dolls are famous in Russia. They are a set of wooden dolls of different sizes, where one is placed inside another. *Matryoshka* comes from the Latin word *mater*, which means "mother". How many *matryoshka* dolls can you draw between the ones below? Make sure that each is slightly bigger than the other.

And don't worry if they don't look the same. Every buddy's design is unique. That's what makes you special!

RAINBOW HUNT

Did you know? South Africa is also called the Rainbow Nation
because of its multiculturalism and the coming together
of different people. Go on a rainbow treasure hunt!
Spot five items for each color of the rainbow around you.
Draw them below and make a rainbow of different objects.

RED

ORANGE

YELLOW

GREEN

BLUE

INDIGO

PURPLE

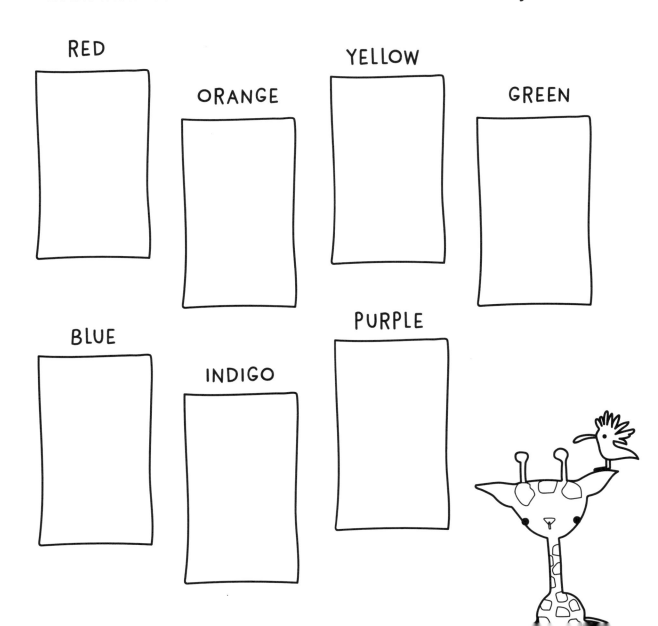

A SECRET MESSAGE

Quipu means "knot" in the language of the Incas in Peru.
Quipus were colored knots, each tied to a main string.
Each different color of knots represented a different item,
while the number of knots represented the quantity of each item.
Draw and color the *quipus* below to show how many potatoes,
onions and carrots each alpaca is carrying. We drew
the knots that represent the potatoes of the left alpaca for you
(but you'll have to color them).

YELLOW: POTATOES
RED: ONIONS
ORANGE: CARROTS

HI FRIEND

Connect the dots and learn how to say "friend"
in different languages.

AMI(E)   FRENCH

DOST   HINDI

SADIQ(A)   ARABIC

RAFIKI   SWAHILI

BEACH DAY

The sun is out and the birds are chirping.
It's a beautiful day in Jamaica. Join Marcia, Marcus
and Gabriella for a delightful time at the beach.

PICNIC TIME

And you can even have a picnic!
Draw everything you'll take with you inside the picnic basket below.

LIKE A FAMOUS ARTIST

Windmills are an iconic symbol of the Netherlands.
Some were so beautiful that famous artists made paintings of them.
Color in the windmills, just like famous artists have.

THE GREAT BAKE

Marielle is feeling generous! She baked a number
of crusty breads and she wants to give them away.
Color in the loaves of bread you want Marielle to set aside for
your friends and family. Add a name tag on each bread
indicating who you're giving the loaves to. We added the first tag.

SOMEONE LOST THE WAY

There's been a mix-up! In the next four pages, something
or someone got trapped in the wrong place.
Color in the drawings except the misplaced
item or animal so that it can escape.

NGORONGORO CRATER
TANZANIA

WHERE AM I?

BRONTE BEACH,
AUSTRALIA

HELP! I'M STUCK

BELGRADE FORTRESS,
SERBIA

LET'S GO ON A TRIP

Manaia and Athena are preparing to go on trips. Help them pack their bags. Color in the different items and draw lines to match them with the appropriate weather and suitcase.

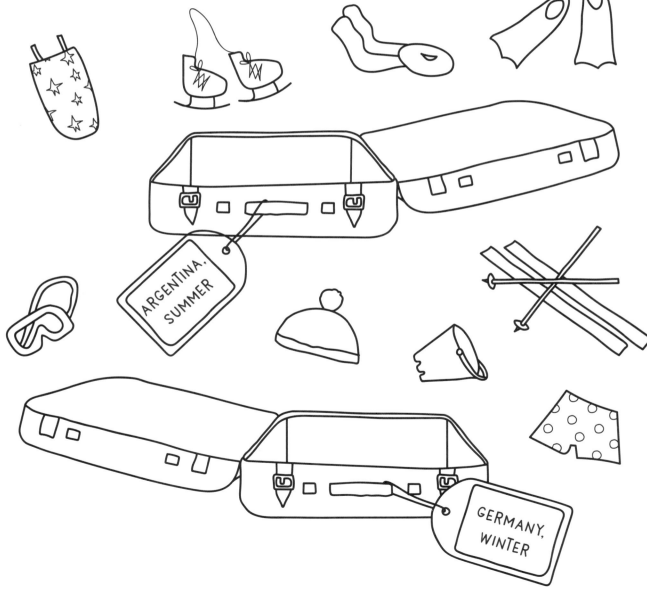

ARGENTINA, SUMMER

GERMANY, WINTER

IT'S DRESS UP TIME

Buddies from around the world have visited Ghana and Kwame has prepared special *kente* shirts for them. *Kente* is a Ghanaian textile made of strips of silk and cotton and colorful patterns, just like Kwame's. Draw *kente* shirts on all the buddies.

DOMINOES OF COLOR

Color in the images so that each tile is linked to the one next to it. The link can be anything you want! For example, if you color the image in the first square pink with blue dots, then the second image can be green with blue dots (connecting factor: blue dots), while the third image can be green with purple stripes (connecting factor: color green).

A FOOTBALL AFFAIR

The Amazon rainforest is home to some incredible animals.
And many of them love to play football in their free time.
Each animal even has its custom-made ball.
Can you match each animal with their football?

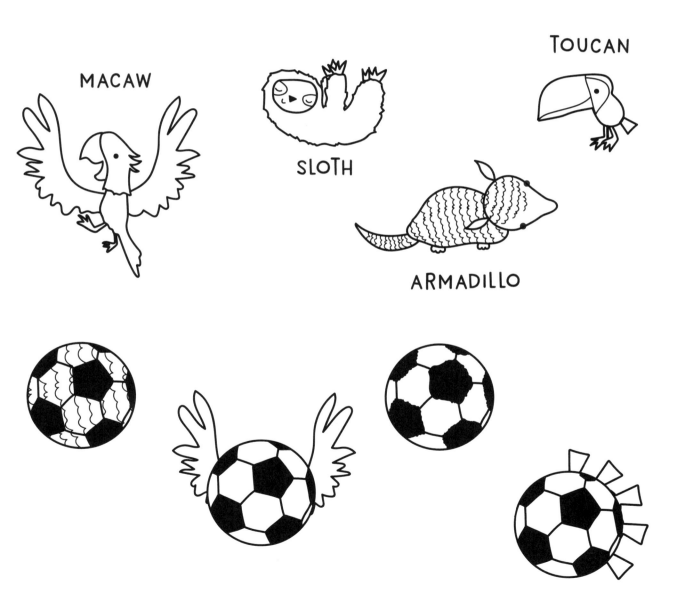

FLAG GAME

Can you color the flag of each country?
You can even add their equivalent stickers in the empty boxes on the right.

5 2	JAPAN
2 ⎢ 2 —5— 2 ⎢ 2	DENMARK
3 1 2	COLOMBIA

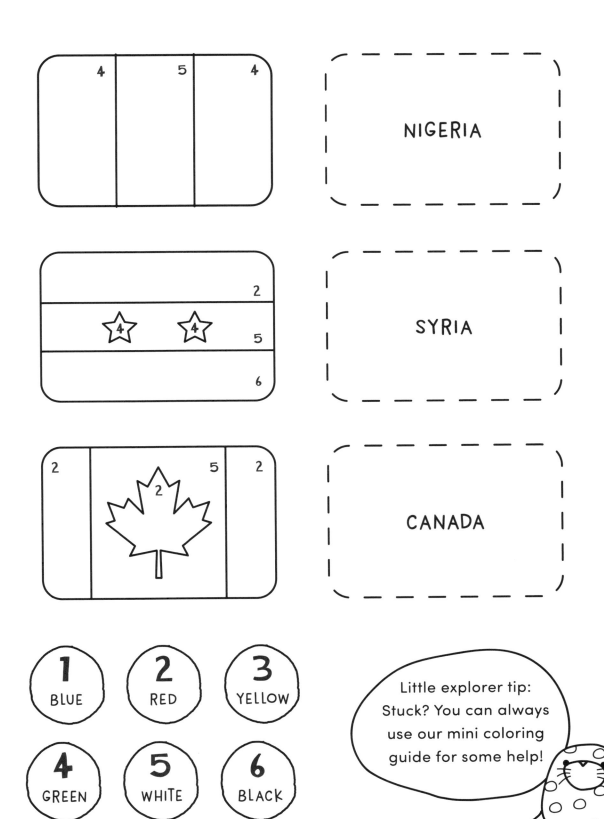

FIND MY HOME

Where does each animal live?

AUSTRALIA

narwhal

JAPAN

rockhopper penguin

CANADA

platypus

TANZANIA

leopard

CHILE

armadillo

BRAZIL

dugong

THE RING TEST

Cashmere is a fiber that is used to make soft, high-quality textiles and clothing. The Kashmir region in India is famous for its production of cashmere shawls! They say that one way to tell whether a shawl is made of 100% cashmere is to perform the ring test: try to pass the shawl through a wedding ring! Help Neha identify the real cashmere shawls by coloring red only the shawls that have passed the ring test.

IMAGINARY SKY CREATURES

The Northern Lights are spectacular lights of different shapes
and colors that can be seen from the sky near the North Pole.
Children love to make stories of monsters out of them.
Think of imaginary sky creatures and draw them.

A MESSAGE TO THE WORLD

Help Akilah protect her home and the Maldives from rising sea levels. Color in the fish and write your ideas and messages on how buddies can protect the environment.

Leaving the room? Please turn off the light!

A BUDDIFUL PATTERN

Color in the buddies and bring them to life!

MY FAMILY TREE

Every one of us has a special story to tell—our background, where our parents, grandparents and other family members come from. Draw your family tree. Don't forget to include all the fluffy members and any friends or anyone else you consider family, too.

YOU CAN BE ANYTHING

Anyone can be a little inventor, a little explorer, a little adventurer or a little dreamer—and imagining it is the first step towards making it come true. What does each mean to you?
Draw yourself below as a ...

 LITTLE INVENTOR

LITTLE EXPLORER

 LITTLE ADVENTURER

LITTLE DREAMER

MAGIC TELESCOPE

If you had a magic telescope that could show you anything around the world, where would you point it at? What would you like to explore? Draw it on the page!

MY COLORING ACTIVITY CHECKLIST

- ◯ HELLO, LITTLE ARTIST!
- ◯ WHAT A WONDERFUL WORLD
- ◯ MATRYOSHKA DOLLS
- ◯ RAINBOW HUNT
- ◯ A SECRET MESSAGE
- ◯ HI FRIEND
- ◯ BEACH DAY
- ◯ PICNIC TIME
- ◯ LIKE A FAMOUS ARTIST
- ◯ THE GREAT BAKE
- ◯ SOMEONE LOST THE WAY
- ◯ WHERE AM I?
- ◯ HELP! I'M STUCK
- ◯ I'M TRAPPED
- ◯ LET'S GO ON A TRIP

- ◯ IT'S STICKER TIME
- ◯ PE-PE-PE-PENGUINS
- ◯ SPOT THE DIFFERENCES
- ◯ IT'S DRESS UP TIME
- ◯ DOMINOES OF COLOR
- ◯ A FOOTBALL AFFAIR
- ◯ FLAG GAME
- ◯ FIND MY HOME
- ◯ THE RING TEST
- ◯ IMAGINARY SKY CREATURES
- ◯ A MESSAGE TO THE WORLD
- ◯ A BUDDIFUL PATTERN
- ◯ MY FAMILY TREE
- ◯ YOU CAN BE ANYTHING
- ◯ MAGIC TELESCOPE

PSST... LET'S GO ON A HUNT! HOW MANY STARS CAN YOU SPOT IN THIS COLORING BOOK?

COMPLETE YOUR COLLECTION, MEET ALL OUR BUDDIES AND EXPLORE THE WORLD!

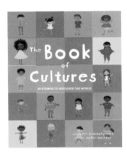

WORLDWIDE
BUDDIES

At Worldwide Buddies, we have created a universe of buddies from different parts of the planet, specially designed for littles to embrace diverse perspectives. Our books and toys take readers on adventures near and far, encouraging them to explore our wonderful world.
Are you ready? Off we go!

LET'S BE BUDDIES!
FOLLOW US / TAG US @WORLDWIDEBUDDIES
WWW.WORLDWIDEBUDDIES.COM

Around the World Coloring Book
Printed in China, first print, 2023